RETIREMENT
LIVING IN FLORIDA

Rosemarie De Gennaro

RETIREMENT
LIVING IN FLORIDA

HIS HEAVEN MY HELL

I Love NY BUT He Loves FL

authorHOUSE®

AuthorHouse™ LLC
1663 Liberty Drive
Bloomington, IN 47403
www.authorhouse.com
Phone: 1-800-839-8640

Published by AuthorHouse   03/07/2014

ISBN: 978-1-4918-6577-4 (sc)
ISBN: 978-1-4918-6576-7 (e)

Library of Congress Control Number: 2014903231

This book is dedicated to all my friends in Florida (you know who you are), especially Mary Jo. They have kept me somewhat sane as I try to live in the Sunshine State.

CONTENTS

INTRODUCTION

So you want to retire to Florida. After all, you have worked hard all your life. You're tired of the North's cold, snowy winters. Most of all, isn't it more affordable than New York?

Let's not forget the self-pity mind-set: how many more years do you have? You deserve it. You were a good worker, parent, grandparent, and a loving spouse. Isn't it your turn? Well, it may be your turn, but what about your better half? Does he or she really want to leave New York, the family, the house that is finally paid off, the beautiful four seasons?

Take it from me—I'm the better half that wants her life back in New York. Before making the big move so the other half can be happy, let's get rid of the myths: The grass is not greener in Florida. In fact, there is no real grass in Florida, just something that resembles New York crabgrass. The only green grass in Florida is on a golf course that you will pay dearly to play.

You may be asking yourself, "Why did this woman consent to relocating to Florida?" It's very simple: I didn't think it would ever happen!

Chapter 1

THE BEGINNING OF THE MOVE

IT ALL STARTED WITH A *Southern Living* home show at the Marriott Hotel on Route 110 in the beautiful town of Huntington, Long Island. A few weeks prior to the show, we received an invitation by mail. You know the type, with two good-looking, grey-haired seniors on the front. They had straight white teeth, sparkling eyes, loving smiles and walked hand in hand along the beach, the sun shining perfectly and a golf course off in the background. Of course, you get these advertisements as you are shoveling snow, cursing the oil company, freezing your butt off as you try to make it to the grocery store on icy roads. Your charge-card bills are just in from the holidays, abundant reminders of how much you spent on your family's gifts and how little they are going to wear the clothes, play with the toys, and enjoy the gift cards.

After receiving and discarding these ads for years, my better half makes a suggestion one Sunday afternoon: let's go and see what it's all

1

about. I had nothing better to do, as the children and grandchildren were busy with sports, as usual. Plus he was going crazy in the house with no football on TV and no golf to play for a couple of months because of the *beautiful* winter weather. *Besides*, I thought to myself, *Mr. Wonderful knows I can't survive in the South, due to the heat.* Somehow, I breathe better in clean, cool, fresh air. I swell like a blimp in the summer months and usually stay at home with the air conditioner cranking day and night. Therefore, Mr. Wonderful would never really move to Florida, a state about which I repeatedly said, "I don't mind visiting, but I could never live there." Believe me, it's not the state; it's just me!

So off we went from our mortgage-free condo in Medford, Long Island, to the *Southern Living* Expo. Just want to reiterate, it was a horrible, cold, icy, rainy day. As we entered this beautiful hotel, we were surrounded by tables and more tables, stacked with brochures showing lovely homes in communities with golf courses, health spas, tennis courts, bocci courts, restaurants, gyms, and pools. Let's not forget those huge banners with the loving, happiest old people in the world. All these apparent Gardens of Eden stretch from Delaware to Florida. Behind the tables are smiling, tanned representatives offering a two-night, three-day stay for bargain prices. Not only can you stay and relax by using all the facilities, but they also provide food, shows, gift certificates, and other freebies. Of course, once you are there, you are obligated to sit down with one of their salespeople, who will give you all sorts of information regarding the community and show you the different models available. They promise it will only take about two hours, and then the rest of the stay you can enjoy and experience the better life. Did I mention they also throw in free golf?

As I squeezed through the crowded room filled with senior citizens, I noticed Mr. Wonderful had several brochures containing information on North Carolina, South Carolina, Virginia, Georgia, and, of course, the Sunshine State of Florida. Out of curiosity, I picked up brochures from Delaware, Pennsylvania, and Maryland.

The talk of a vacation began. After speaking with several representatives from various states, somehow it began to seem feasible to get out of the cold and take advantage of their getaways. We didn't have to make a definite date; there was no deposit or commitment. All we had to do was fill out a postcard with our name, address, and phone number. Sounds harmless, but it truly was the beginning of the move.

Chapter 2

THE HARMLESS DISCUSSION

O N OUR DRIVE BACK HOME, we commented on the beauty of the homes, the cheaper taxes, the amenities, and, of course, the lower prices compared to New York. We both agreed it sure would be hard to leave family and friends, especially our grandchildren whom we saw almost on a daily basis. We decided we would, sometime in the future maybe, map out a vacation from North Carolina to Florida and take advantage of the mini-vacations that were being offered. It all seemed so simple. I would go home and place all the brochures in a desk drawer, and that would be that.

A few days after the show, salespeople from Delaware to Florida started to call. All of them had reduced the prices on the mini-vacations, and some had slashed prices on their homes. I would politely explain that the timing was not right and I would get back to them. Every day I would receive several pieces of mail from different states. A few weeks later a salesperson would call to make sure we received the mail and to ask when we could "come on down." This went on for months. No matter how nicely or nastily I spoke to them, they still kept calling and mailing. No matter how many times I said, "Don't call me, I'll call you," they stayed on their mission to get us.

Chapter 3

A REPRIEVE

SPRING FINALLY ARRIVED! MY HUSBAND was happy again. He was playing golf and felt better now that it was getting warmer and we were getting out of the house more. *Ah, I'm safe*, I'd think. There was very little talk of moving. The economy and housing market weren't looking too great. Condos weren't selling, and neighbors who sunk money into renovating theirs weren't getting their asking price.

I was a lot calmer—so calm that I decided to join a local senior citizen center. After all, I was sixty and finally qualified. I knew quite a few of these seniors, some from our condo complex, others from church, and many from bus trips I organized to Atlantic City, Foxwoods, New York City shows, and other mini-vacation spots. I really enjoyed their company. Unfortunately, a few weeks after joining this group, I broke my ankle while leaving the center. My friends immediately called 911. An ambulance arrived and transported me to the hospital, and I had surgery the following morning.

Now, guess who was stuck with me in the house from April until June. Since I was confined to a wheelchair and had to use a walker to literally hop from bedroom to bathroom to kitchen, I was no longer answering the phone or able to retrieve the mail. As the weeks went by, my husband was doing everything for me. I was very grateful but getting frustrated. I'm not one to just sit around the house, and he was starting to get antsy. His famous line to neighbors and family was "She broke her ankle, but I'm the one suffering." All were amused except me. Now that he was receiving the brochures and talking to the agents, he was getting more interested in moving to the South. With all the support that I had been getting from my family and friends, I did not want to move at all.

After six long weeks, I was finally rid of the cast and wheelchair and got around by using the walker. I could finally shower and put light pressure on my foot. Home therapy was really a blessing. My husband was able to play golf at the nine-hole course at our condo. We both enjoyed the break. However, as he was playing golf, more and more snowbirds (residents who either vacation or have a second home down South for the winter months) were coming home. Now, winter in New York in 2009 was pretty horrible, even for me. November through March had weeks on end with snow, ice, and cold temperatures. April and May had more than the usual number of rainy days. Our snowbird neighbors were glad they were not in New York during that time and made sure to inform us of this every time we saw them.

My husband had a golf buddy who owned a home in Florida. His buddy planned to go down the first two weeks in June and asked my husband to see his place. My husband could stay for two weeks and use all the amenities, and the two of them could visit some of the communities that we had talked about at the expo.

I really felt this would be a nice vacation for my husband, as he had been doing so much for me. My children and neighbors were willing to assist me while he was gone. I also thought he would come back and abandon the idea of relocating. I thought he would realize there's no place like home, and I hoped he would miss not only family but everything New York has to offer.

After a few discussions, he decided to go to Florida for only one week. Maybe he would like our friend's community, and we could add that on our list of places to vacation.

Well, he went. He had a great time, fell in love with the community, and couldn't wait until I was able to travel. As usual, I ignored the whole conversation. I had at least four more months of therapy on my ankle, and the housing market was getting worse. Even the government's tax credit for first-time buyers didn't seem to be helping. I could not think about this half-baked idea. I had enough to worry about, like walking pain free!

During the very hot months of June, July, August, and September, my husband continued to assist me and take me to doctors. He also took me to the physical therapist three times a week. It was during that time I experienced pain from a cyst on my back that I had for years. I didn't realize how much it had grown in recent months. Wouldn't you know it, when I had fallen and broken my ankle I also ruptured the cyst's capsule. Another operation was performed in October. Thank God it was out-patient surgery.

Some weeks later, we decided we both needed a vacation, and out came the brochures. Reservations for the inexpensive getaways were made, and my husband also booked a mini-cruise to Nassau leaving from Florida. *Oh my God. Please help me,* I thought. I not only couldn't stand the thought of moving to Florida, I was also one of those people who fear taking cruises. *This can't be happening!*

Things couldn't have been more depressing for me when I receive a postcard in the mail from a local real estate agent. You've guessed it:

before we left for Florida and the cruise, we signed up with the agent "just to test the waters." Let's face it: nobody was really buying. The economy was getting worse every day, the Obama credit had expired, and my neighbors' homes, which were much nicer than mine, were not selling. If they couldn't sell their homes, how could I sell mine? Besides, the holidays and bad weather were right around the corner. *What's the worry?* I told myself. *We'll get this southern vacation, cruise, and real estate project settled so we can get on with our lives.*

Chapter 4

TIME TO WORRY

TEN DAYS BEFORE THANKSGIVING WE were off on my husband's dream vacation and my never ending nightmare. I really had no choice. You must understand that my husband hates to fly. However, over the years, on special anniversaries or my birthday he would get up enough nerve to fly. In order to make me happy, he flew to Europe, Las Vegas, New Mexico, California, and a few other places. So now it was my turn to return the favor. I must tell you, I was not as gracious as he. I complained from day one, and I never really stopped.

Our first stop was North Carolina, followed by South Carolina. We both agreed the communities were excellent but not what we really wanted. Besides, if I was going to sweat to death, I might as well consider Florida, where he really wanted to be.

So we visited our friend's community in Florida. We had been in contact with a salesperson from this community, and he made arrangements for us to spend a few days in one of their rentals.

This community was a golfer's dream. The place was huge with several golf courses, restaurants, and amenities galore. It had shopping, churches, doctors' offices, hospitals, town squares, movie houses, and much more. You name it, they had it. You really didn't need a second car, as you could get to everything by golf cart. Sounds great, right? I found it too congested. The traffic was ridiculous, and the snowbirds hadn't even arrived yet. Everybody seemed to have a golf cart. They were all over the place. Do you know what it is like to drive your car behind those personalized golf carts? Half of those seniors lost their licenses years ago. Imagine driving behind and around Mr. Magoo! It was the perfect place to develop road rage. The drivers were road hogs and simply refused to get to the side of the road. Some of them went so slow, while others would speed. There was no happy medium. In order to get from one end of this community to another, it could take thirty minutes. There was an accident or two every week.

This community had plenty of stores every couple of miles. However, they were the same stores over and over again. Dancing and listening to a band at one of their squares was a nightly event. This so-called entertainment started with a happy hour at five o'clock. Trust me, you need a drink to see this, and I give these people credit. They were truly enjoying themselves dancing and singing under the stars until ten o'clock. I, on the other hand, felt like I was back in a 1960s disco with polyester seniors. Either these folks were reliving their past or they never had one. I hadn't heard those pick-up lines in decades.

One night, as my husband left me for a few moments to purchase a soda, an older guy sat next to me. I rolled my eyes to the heavens and asked, "Why me, Lord?"

Sure enough this gentleman proceeded to give me an astronomy lesson: "Look over here—that's Orion. Look over there—that's the brightest star."

Finally, I said, "Look over to your right—that's my husband." Needless to say, they started talking about sports, the wonderful community, and the great state of Florida. My husband had a wonderful time and couldn't wait to see the model homes.

The next morning we met the salesperson. He was very nice and wanted to make sure we were enjoying the house that he had reserved for us. It really was beautiful, and they even supplied tasty snacks and breakfast treats. Then it was time to see the models. Of course, the house we were staying in was out of our price range. After looking at several smaller models, we inquired about one home that was in our budget. As much as we liked it, I was informed that we could not make any changes to the floor plan or accessories. The locals call these "cookie-cutter" houses. I didn't care for the carpeting, and when I asked if I could upgrade to hardwood flooring, the answer was "No." However, once I purchased the home, they could rip up the carpeting, and I could have one of their men install the flooring. In other words, you have to pay for carpeting in the sale price, rip it up, and then pay for flooring. Couldn't I get a credit for the carpet and pay the difference for the flooring? The answer was still "No." Additionally, I felt the vinyl siding work was shoddy. So I asked, "If I'm not happy with the siding, would they change it to my satisfaction?" Again, the answer was "No, this is the quality."

The seller also wanted $10,000 added to the price of the house for maintenance of the common areas. This was above the regular home owner's association fees. *Are you kidding me?* I looked at my husband and said, "We're out of here." I refused to live in a congested, senior citizen Disneyland with Mr. Magoos riding in golf carts. We left the next morning to catch the ship to Nassau.

Chapter 5

THE CRUISE

OH BOY, LOOK AT THE size of this cruise liner! *Help, I don't want to go! Where are all these people going?* I simply don't understand the concept of a cruise. I have to get on a ship built like a hotel casino and float for four days in the middle of the ocean. Why? I can stay on land in a beautiful, large room; dine; swim; shop; gamble; and not worry about seasickness, hurricanes, or, more importantly, drowning.

After checking in and receiving pills for nausea, we proceeded to our so-called suite. *What the heck is this? This can't be the suite we upgraded to. If this was the upgraded suite, how small can the other one be? Didn't we pay extra for a porthole? Why didn't they say the lifeboat would be blocking it? Hey, only one side of the bed has entry, and it's not my side! Oh, I see, I have to crawl from the bottom of the bed to my pillow every night. This is just lovely. However, it is not as lovely as the so-called bathroom. Oh, look at this small closet they turned into a bathroom. You can do your business, shower, and shave at the same time. How convenient!*

Before we knew it, we had to leave the luxury of our room as the captain was speaking and wanted all of us on deck to explain what we must do in case of an emergency. I felt like I was on a cheap Titanic. As I looked at all the people unable to follow directions, I realized if anything went wrong, it would be total chaos. I wanted to go home.

I had been on the ship for two hours listening to calypso music and watching women of varying sizes in bikinis made for size-two models when a passenger informed me that this was the day a rocket shuttle would launch from Cape Canaveral. *Oh my God. They are all going to the same side of the ship! I can't believe I'm nauseous and tired of the music and the people already; we are still at the dock!*

Well, the launch was beautiful, successful, and I was excited to eyewitness the event. Maybe this cruise would not be as horrible as I was anticipating . . . . Wrong! We no sooner set sail when we started experiencing rough waters due to a tropical hurricane. Wonderful! As the calypso band continued to play and the ship rocked from side to side, my husband informed me it was time for dinner. Of course, I didn't have much of an appetite or desire to meet anyone. Luckily we were seated with very nice people. After introductions, we learned four were from Florida and two from North Carolina. They had all been on several cruises and stated this was the rockiest they had ever experienced. As we were conversing and perusing the menus, our waiter introduced himself. I must admit all the waiters were gracious, professional, and very accommodating. The food was plentiful, but I couldn't eat between the nausea and the discussions about the merits of moving to Florida or North Carolina. All I wanted to do was get off the ship and go home.

After dinner, I skipped the show and decided to try my luck at the slots in the gambling room. It's amazing, but usually I forget about everything when I play the slots. However, this time I found it hard to forget I was on a cruise as I swayed to and fro, concentrating on keeping my balance on the stool. I managed to break even around 2:00 a.m. and found my way back to our suite. Now I had to figure out how to wash, brush, and get to bed. To be truthful, washing, brushing, and getting changed in the tiny bathroom was easier than sitting on the stool at the slot machine. The closeness of the walls contained my swaggering and afforded me the ability to accomplish my tasks. However, getting on my side of the bed from the foot to the pillow was not a pretty sight.

This routine lasted for two days and nights until we docked in Nassau. I was so happy to see land. I couldn't wait to get off the ship, walk around, and visit the Atlantis Casino. *Wow, one whole day on land until 9:00 p.m.* But no! My husband was on land for approximately two hours when he informed me he wasn't too impressed, didn't want to go shopping, and had absolutely no intention of gambling or staying on the island. So we returned to the ship, the calypso music, and the ship's small casino. After a nice dinner and show, we went back to the suite to try to get a good night's rest. Unfortunately, we sailed all night through a horrible storm. The lifeboat kept rocking closer to the porthole, my head kept banging the wall, and I really had to stop myself from doing harm to my husband, who was sleeping like a baby.

Finally it was the last day of the cruise. After breakfast, we were out of there.

Chapter 6

A BEAUTIFUL COMMUNITY

NEXT WE WERE OFF TO the Florida community that we both knew we couldn't afford. We planned to listen to the spiel and enjoy three days at the beautiful place.

The community was really top shelf. When we walked into the sales office, it was as if we were in a millionaire's study. The furniture, draperies, and decor were exquisite. When the agent drove us to our condo, the landscaping, pools, golf courses, and restaurants on the way were absolutely amazing. The condo that we stayed in was truly fit for a king.

After visiting models that were absolutely beautiful and well constructed, my husband and I realized they were well worth the price but not in our budget. Therefore, we decided to enjoy the better life for a few days and then go back to New York to enjoy Thanksgiving with our children.

As happy as I was to leave Florida and end the vacation from hell, my husband was disappointed by not being able to move to this community. But he was still hopeful we would sell our condo and retire to Florida, his golf heaven. On our way out of the community, I quietly said a prayer to myself. I needed a sign from above as to what to do in this situation. Sure enough, a few miles down the road we saw a huge white billboard that read in bold black letters, "Eternity in Hell Is a Long Time." *Oh, you've got to be kidding!* I thought. Was it possible I was going to move to this place? No way! It was just God's way of joking with me. Sometimes I think He created me for His amusement.

Chapter 7

HOME FOR THE HOLIDAYS

AH, WE WERE BACK IN New York. It looked so great. It truly felt like Thanksgiving. No more palm trees, no more eighty-degree weather, and everyone was so miserable looking for the right turkey—it was good to be home.

We celebrated Thanksgiving with our children and grandchildren. I had so much to be thankful for: I was back in New York with family, our condo wasn't selling, and the buzz for Florida was over. I had kept my promise by going to Florida and checking it out. I made it through the cruise. Maybe things could finally get back to normal. Not so fast!

One day, as I was decorating the house for Christmas, the phone rang. It was the real estate agent from Florida calling not only to wish us a Merry Christmas but also to inform us that the model we loved would be available in March and would be sold with all the bells and whistles for the original price. That was great, I explained, but we still couldn't afford it. I also explained that we didn't have a buyer for our condo. I wished her a merry Christmas and a happy New Year and said I would call her if there were any changes in our circumstances.

Christmas was absolutely wonderful. We had a few people look at the condo in December but had no serious buyers. Floridian real estate agents stopped calling. The children and grandchildren were excited and filled the house with life. *Gee, I think I am finally at peace*, I thought. *Happy New Year!*

Chapter 8

HAPPY NEW YEAR 2010

I N New York, the month of January 2010 was really brutal. I
had to agree with my husband, the cold was bone chilling. We
were really getting a lot of snow that year, and he was getting the Florida
bug again. I patiently told him to calm down. "We looked and we can't
do a thing until we sell the condo," I said. "Maybe someday we can be
snowbirds, but not now. After all, we are only sixty. We have time."

I no sooner said, "Calm down," when our Long Island real estate
agent called. I couldn't believe it. It was a terribly cold Sunday afternoon,
and someone wanted to see our condo. What could I do but say "Fine"?
Sure enough, this woman entered my condo with measuring tape in
hand. It seemed she had always wanted to live in our complex since she
was a child. She had babysat in this place when it was first established
in the 1970s. She was determined to live here. She had been looking at
many resales for a couple of years but never found the right one. She
proceeded to measure counter tops, the refrigerator area, and windows

as she spoke of bringing her husband the following week so they could both measure and make sure their things would fit.

I looked at my agent, wondering if this person was truly serious or just wanted something to do on this dreary day. My agent later explained to me that she remembered this woman from many open houses. She wondered whether this woman would ever purchase a condo but believed this time the woman might be serious. As my husband was smiling, I was getting nervous. I kept recalling the billboard I had seen at the last community we visited in Florida: "Eternity in Hell Is a Long Time."

Well, as my bad luck goes, my husband got some good luck! We signed the contract in February, and if all went well with the financial papers, we were to have a potential closing date sometime in April before the government incentive was to expire. I guess I was in denial because I kept hoping something would happen to prevent the sale. As time went on, reality hit me. So when my husband and I discussed the possible move, I compromised and agreed to rent a home in Florida for six months. If we both liked it and if I could visit New York whenever I felt I needed to, then we would purchase a home. However, if I couldn't take the change, we would pack our bags and return to New York. Since we agreed to this compromise and the sale was not final, I managed to cope during February and the first part of March. Then our lawyer called and informed us that the closing date was May 5. This meant the buyers would get the government credit, and, should we decide to purchase a home in Florida, we would not get that benefit. While I realized this fact, I didn't care much; I thought we'd just rent a place and move back to New York.

Chapter 9

WHAT TO DO

WHAT ARE WE GOING TO *do now? The condo is sold! What do I do with my furniture? Where am I going to live? How will I say good-bye to my children, grandchildren, family, and friends? This is insane! More importantly, how come my husband is so happy while I am so miserable?*

After much discussion, we decided to give our furniture to family members and donate whatever they did not want. I even donated my car. Our personal items, which consisted of over forty boxes, would be stored in relatives' attics until we could decide whether we were coming or going. The cost to transport these items to Florida would have been too expensive.

Our friend who had a home in Florida offered us the opportunity to rent it for a few months until we could find a place of our own. The worst part would be saying good-bye. It was one big crying session, from family to friends to acquaintances. I hadn't realized that so many would take our move as hard as I was. It was beautiful, but painful at the same time.

Chapter 10

HOMELESS

I T WAS SOON TIME FOR the closing on our condo. I cried, my husband was overjoyed, the buyers were very happy, and both lawyers were looking at me as if I was crazy. The closing went off without a glitch, and we returned to our jam-packed car and headed to Florida.

I was in a daze all the way down I-95. It was the longest two days of travelling I had spent. When we arrived at our friend's house, I was pleasantly surprised. It was beautiful, and I really wanted to just stay there for awhile. My husband loved this community from when he had visited it last year. I, on the other hand, loved to visit, but not to purchase. So, in my mind, we'd just rent, relax, and go back to New York in a few months. I truly believed my husband would never be able to stay away from his children and grandchildren.

No sooner had we gotten settled when our agent from the Florida community we loved but could not afford called my husband's cell phone. I've always hated cell phones! It seemed that, due to the economy, the purchase prices for these homes had been reduced. She also informed us that the model we had really liked was up for sale, including all the furniture and furnishings. She asked if we were still interested. You can imagine my husband's response and my anguish. Of course, this community was only two miles from that "Eternity in Hell Is a Long Time" sign. As I heard him speak so excitedly and courteously to the agent, I tried to signal him not to make an appointment so soon. Really, we had barely unpacked our clothes! I reminded him of our compromise. We were to rent this house, look at all areas, and see if we really wanted to live in Florida. He looked at my face, listened to my whispers, and explained to our agent that we were not ready to buy but would see her soon.

A few days later, the agent called again to see if we wanted to make an appointment to visit the community and take a second look at the model. We had only been in Florida one week, and I realized we had been spending money as if we were on vacation. I started to wonder how much we would spend if we continued to rent for six months and live this way. This was not good. We could end up with very little money to purchase a home back in New York. Under the circumstances, I agreed with my husband to meet the agent and revisit the community.

Chapter 11

THE REVISIT

THERE WE WERE, BACK IN the classy community. The place was as gorgeous as we had remembered it being. Our agent was as gracious as always. After a brief discussion of the sale of our condo and our plans to rent for awhile, we were off to see the model. As we drove through the beautiful surroundings, I explained how much I wanted to return to New York. Our agent informed us that many people are homesick at first, but within three months the majority change their minds and just love Florida. I have never been known to be part of the majority; I was not convinced. She focused more on my husband, who had a smile cemented on his face. They spoke of the great weather, the sun, the golf, the wonderful community, the people, and all the upscale amenities. I sat in the backseat of the car cursing the heat, the golf, and wanting to wipe the smile off my husband's face. However, I kept these thoughts to myself. I just remained quiet and kept thinking, *this too shall pass*.

As we approached the model, which was beautifully landscaped and on a golf course plot, I could see my husband was in golf heaven. Our agent unlocked the front door, and the house was beautiful. The professional decorator did an amazing job. The window treatments and draperies complimented the expensive furniture and artwork. The model had upgrades in every room, especially in the kitchen and bathrooms. There were enough knickknacks to furnish two homes. The artificial plants and fixtures accented each room perfectly. After we toured the whole place, my husband was definitely hooked. Now it was time for the agent to reel him in. It wasn't hard to do. The price of the home was reduced $20,000. Since the model was already on the golf course, they would not charge us the usual extra $20,000 for a golf-course lot. That in itself was a savings of $40,000. She already told us they were including the furniture and furnishings. My husband was ready to seal the deal when I interjected that we would have to think about it and explore a bit more. The agent drove us back to our car and suggested that we make a list of things we would want to make this home "our own." She would give us a call in a few days just to see if we were still interested and if we had made a "wish list." We agreed and went on our merry way.

As my husband and I drove back to our rental, he remarked that he couldn't believe how much the price had dropped. He imagined living in this beautiful home on the golf course. Considering it was completely furnished, all we needed were a washer, dryer, refrigerator, and TV, made it more feasible. All we really had to do was go back to New York to pick up our clothes and personal items. "This really seemed like a great opportunity", he said. Before he got too carried away, I reminded him that we had only been in Florida one week. I was willing to research this more by looking at other homes. "But let's remember we compromised to rent for a few months before making any definite decision," I said. He agreed he was rushing into it and we should stop by a real estate office to view other properties. In the meantime, he requested that I make a list as our agent suggested. I agreed, and I decided to make a list of demands that would be very difficult to meet.

Chapter 12

SCOUTING

THE FOLLOWING MORNING, WE STARTED our research by visiting other communities. The models were beautiful, the communities had plenty amenities, but the quality of the homes were not even close to the home we had been offered. Although the prices were lower, we figured by the time we added the upgrades and furniture, these homes would cost more than the one we really liked. Over the next few days, we went to a real estate office and asked for resales. We explained our situation and were very truthful about the model we were being offered. Again we saw homes that needed a little TLC that were less costly. But again, once we added repairs, appliances, painting, and furniture, the homes would cost more than the new move-in model. One real estate agent could not believe we were getting such a good deal at this particular well-known community. So, being me, I showed her the place. She looked at my husband and advised us to grab it now. We went back to her office, and she showed us all the homes that were recently sold and the ones that were still on the market. She admitted that we were getting a great deal and she, being a multiple listing agent, had nothing to show us further.

We went to several open houses during the week. Nothing compared to the deal we had been offered. We were convinced if we were going to buy anything, it should be the original home we truly liked with all the bells and whistles.

Although we had only been in Florida for about three weeks, I checked our finances, and our account balance was going down rapidly. I was getting cornered. I wondered, *Should I stick to my guns and rent another five months, leaving us very short to purchase something back home? Or should I bite the bullet and purchase the house as an investment with hopes of selling it within a year or so?* I was starting to go crazy tossing these ideas back and forth in my head over and over again. I had to make a decision, if simply for my own peace of mind.

In the meantime, I made a wish list that I believed had no chance of being fulfilled. Perhaps this would be my way out. I would show our agent this insane list, and she would tell us it could not be met. The deal would be squashed, and in a few weeks I would be on my way back to New York.

Chapter 13

THE PLAN

L IKE CLOCKWORK, THE PHONE RANG the following morning. It was
our agent inquiring if we made our wish list. Feeling confident,
I explained we would see the house once more and find out if we could
come to an agreement on the list. She was very pleased, and we met the
next day. I felt sure my demands would not be met.

On entering the house, I skipped the small talk and went straight to
my demands. We started with the kitchen. I noted that above the range
hung a hood but no microwave. Could we have a microwave installed?
"No problem," she said. We really needed appliances. Could we have a
refrigerator, washer and dryer installed? I noticed some small items could
be added in the bathrooms and asked if they could be supplied. Well, they
could supply the appliances and items by giving us a $5,000 allowance,
she told me. We could also choose to purchase any appliance or item on
the list on our own as long as we stayed within the $5,000. If the cost
was less, we could deduct the difference from the sale price of the house.

I looked at the large lanai and explained I would want it screened in with an outside door and an outside fan. "No problem," she said again. I noted I would need a fan in the living room as well. "No problem." I requested to keep all the beddings, linens, towels, accessories, artwork, and every knickknack. "No problem." I expressed that I really did not care for the master bedroom furniture and the dining room set. "No problem." We could switch the furniture from another model.

I started to worry since all the demands were being met, so I thought I would bring out the big guns and ask for the price to be reduced. To my shock and horror, she agreed. My last hope was to request an extension on the sale promotion, which was free golf until the year 2015. "No problem, you can extend it to the year 2025," she said.

I looked at my husband, who once again wore a grin, and asked him for any suggestions that I may have forgotten. Of course, he was no help. He just told the agent to give him the papers to sign.

I recommended we think about it a little more before signing a contract and leaving a deposit. Once again she agreed to note on all paperwork that the sale was pending for three days. If another buyer wanted the house, she would call, and we would have to give her a decision. If not, we had three days to either come to the office, sign the contract, and leave a 10 percent deposit or let her know we were not interested. The solution seemed very fair, so we shook hands and went on our way.

Needless to say, I was somewhat relieved. I was hoping another person would want the home with fewer demands than I did. That way the home would be sold, I could continue renting for another month or two, and all would be just fine. What I was not anticipating was my husband's excitement. He believed we got the sale of the century. He was impressed with my list and my price haggling. I reminded him we still had three days to reconsider and shop for appliances.

The next day, we went to every appliance store you could imagine. After all was said and done, we found appliances and the extra items I had requested at a lower price than the $5,000 allowance. Perhaps this could be my ace in the hole. I would request $5,000 off the sale price of the house and purchase aforementioned on my own. I also remembered there was a $2,000 deposit for amenities that would be reimbursed to us should we sell the home. Maybe I would bargain to pay only $1,000 for the membership and pay for only half the closing costs. Surely these extra demands would squash the deal. Of course, I could always just walk away from this deal, but then I was back to my original dilemma of renting, spending money, and having nothing to show for it. I was so confused!

When I am confused I pray for guidance and a sign. God never lets me down. I know some people think this is crazy, but a person of faith does not. A person of non-faith may call it coincidence, good luck, serendipity, or just plain "whatever." Whenever I ask for a sign, I need it in black and white. I'm not much for looking at the abstract and figuring out the meaning. I am a simple person with simple requests requiring simple answers.

After praying with all my heart and soul, I requested to meet a person with the same name as mine, with the exact spelling. It sounds nuts, but that was what I needed to continue this venture. I am very proud of my name, as I am named after my grandmother, Rosemarie. I am not named Rose, Rose Marie, Rose Mary, or Rosemary. If anyone ever calls me Rosemary, I remind them I am not an herb. Believe it or not, I have met more women with the spelling variations. I told my husband my plan. At first he looked at me like I was ridiculous. That was until I reminded him that I prayed for a sign before I married him, and here we were forty-four years later.

You see, when we got engaged in 1968, we were both very young. However, at that time, being engaged at nineteen years of age was not that uncommon. This was especially true if you came from an Italian background. I remember my parents saying, "Hey, you better hurry up and get married. If you're not married by twenty-one, you'll probably be single the rest of your life." Of course, I never worried about this, as I enjoyed being single. I loved working two jobs and going out on the weekends with my friends to the local disco. I really enjoyed dancing and meeting people. However, my husband joined the navy right after high school. When he learned he was being stationed in Maine for a year, he wanted to marry me so we could be together. As much as I wanted to be with him, I also wanted to remain single for awhile. Again, I was very confused. So I went to Mass and prayed fervently for a sign. Leaving the church, I went to the bank across the street to cash my paycheck. Back in the day, there were no ropes to follow for the next teller. You just waited on a line for the teller of your choice. As I went to the line of my choice and waited for the teller, a woman in her sixties was standing before me. After a minute or so, she turned around and asked, "Miss, can you do me a favor? This is my husband's first social security check. Unfortunately, I left my reading glasses in the car, and I can't remember the exact amount of the check. Could you please read it for me so I know I will be receiving the right amount?" She could have asked the person in front of her or next to her. However, she turned around and asked for my assistance. Well, I had no idea that once I agreed to read the check I would receive my sign, right there in black and white. The check was written to "Mr. Louis De Gennaro," the exact spelling of my husband's name. I could not believe my eyes. I looked at her in amazement and exclaimed, "You are Mrs. Louis De Gennaro? I am to be Mrs. Louis De Gennaro," and explained my apprehensions. She put her arms around me and said, "Oh, don't worry. If your Louie is anything like my Louie, he will be a wonderful husband and father. We have been married for forty-six years, and even though I have had to work to make ends meet, I would do it all over again." It was absolutely remarkable; I always knew my Louie would be a great husband and father, but I also knew I would have to work in order to make the bills. As we parted, we hugged, and she wished me good luck and happiness. As I left the bank, I looked up to the heavens and said, "Okay, if that is what God wants, I will do His will." This memory has so comforted me during the good and bad times. Now I was focusing on it again.

After a long day of appliance shopping and driving in the heat, I just wanted to go back to our rental, say my prayers, and go to sleep. After all, tomorrow would be day two of my decision making and looking for a sign.

The next morning we decided to look at more models, scout the area, and find a local bank. There had been no meeting of a Rosemarie. With the exploring over, it was time to open bank accounts in Florida. Right across from our rental home was a shopping area with several streets dedicated to every bank you can think of. My husband looked at me and advised me to pick one. I figured while I was trusting in God, we might as well go to the bank that had "trust" in its name. We walked in, and Rosemarie greeted us at the door. "Hi. Welcome to our bank. As you can see by my name tag, my name is Rosemarie. Is there anything I can help you with this morning?" I looked at my husband and advised him that he had won again.

He responded by saying, "I never had a doubt." We explained to Rosemarie that we may be purchasing a home shortly and needed to establish accounts. She was very professional, and before you knew it, we had savings and checking accounts ready to go for the next day, if needed. I still found it mind-boggling. My first answer to a prayer came from a patron on a bank line in 1968, and now I received another answer from a bank clerk. During my life I have received many signs to guide me. I am grateful for the blessings.

Chapter 14

THE CONTRACT

ALL MY PLANS HAD BACKFIRED except the prayer for a sign. Somehow this escapade started with a sign, "Eternity in Hell Is a Long Time," and now appeared to be ending with one, Rosemarie. I figured I might as well go for broke and request my new demands before they showed us the contract.

Our agent greeted us with a smile and contract in hand. As I read it with tears in my eyes, I noticed the $2,000 deposit, which would be refunded to us in the event we sold the house. I also noticed that the closing fees were higher than anticipated. The $5,000 allowance for appliances was in the contract as well. In regard to my wish list, all was written as I had listed.

As I took the pen to sign, I told our agent I could not sign unless I only paid $1,000 for the deposit, she removed the $5,000 allowance and took it out of the purchase price, and the seller would pay half the closing costs. My husband and the agent looked at me as if I had completely lost my mind. I could not have cared less, and I put the pen down. She told us that she would have to discuss this with her employer. I said I understood, and as she left the room, my husband just glared at me in disbelief. As we awaited her return, my husband said I was asking for too much and asked what I would do if they said no. I explained to him how much I did not want to live in Florida. If they said no, we would enjoy this vacation for a little while longer. We would then return to New York and look for a small house. On the other hand, if they agreed to my terms, I promised to sign the papers and hope for the best.

About fifteen minutes passed, and our agent came to us shaking her head and smiling. She informed us that a new contract would be written, congratulated us on our new home, and asked us to lunch. After lunch we would come back to the office sign the new contract and leave a deposit. We could be in our new home in two weeks. I was baffled, but I humbly agreed. What else could I do? I never go back on my word. I did all I could to negate the deal yet keep my promise to try living in Florida. Two signs were given to me: "Eternity in Hell Is a Long Time" and my meeting of a person who had the exact name as mine. Who would have guessed?

As the three of us ate lunch and discussed the contract, I never saw two happier people than my husband and my agent. They both tried to cheer me up by telling me what a great deal I had made and that all would be well. I couldn't swallow the lunch, or their advice. About an hour had passed, and it was time to return to the office and sign the contract. All was in order. We signed, left a deposit, and were told the closing date would be May 25, 2010.

My husband and I immediately left the office and ventured over to the "Tag Office." Up north we call it the Department of Motor Vehicles. To our surprise it also was the Tax Assessor Building. It was really amazing that a building the size of a large cafeteria housed both agencies.

We had always heard that home taxes and car insurance were cheaper in Florida. It was true, but not really. You see, in order to qualify for the Homestead Act, you must file by March. Since this was now May, we did not qualify. However, we could apply now and receive the reduction for next year. This would have been a savings of approximately $400. In New York we were receiving a larger discount on my taxes due to my husband's veteran status and the Star Program, a program similar to the Homestead Act. Therefore, we would now be paying about $500 in taxes more than we were paying in our condo. If we had lived in a one-family home on Long Island, we would have saved thousands of dollars. At least that appeared to be true at the time. However, if you consider that, in Florida, you pay a monthly fee for sewer usage, water, and garbage pickup, the savings is not as much as you would have anticipated. The sewer and water is very expensive compared to Long Island. I find this ironic since the water tastes horrible. The water is so hard that when you take a shower, it just isn't the same. This water also does a job on your clothes. Once again you will spend money on purchasing drinking water or choosing to buy an expensive water filtration system. In Florida, they urge you to be very conservative on water use. This is simply impossible because the water pipes cannot be placed deep into the ground. Why? Florida is basically a swamp. In order to have cold water you must run the tap for at least three minutes. After that time you can have a glass of horrible-tasting, somewhat cool water. Don't even bother to attempt to do a load of clothes in cold water. Set the washing machine to the cold wash cycle, and you will receive very warm water. On the other hand, should you want really hot water, let the water run at least two minutes. This was the result of our water situation, even after we purchased an energy-saving hot-water-on-demand device. You can't make this stuff up.

Now it was time to look for car insurance. I must admit the car insurance was about half the cost of a New York policy. However, who knew that registering a car in Florida would be so expensive? Would you believe it cost us $570? We had just purchased the car a few months prior to our move and paid New York registration and sales tax. It didn't make a difference. Another important fact to know is that you have to "hand deliver" your old plates to the Department of Motor Vehicles. The "Tag Office" would not mail them back. After I forked over the $570, the person assisting us inquired about the month of my birth date. As I mentioned, it was now the month of May. I told her I was born in September. She proceeded to get our plates and receipts and then informed me that in the State of Florida, registration renewal would be due in September, the month of my birth. I could not believe this and asked her why she didn't inform me before payment. I explained my husband's birthday was in April, and at least using his birthday we could have had a longer period of time before renewing the registration. She apologized. An apology was nice, but it didn't equal the savings we could have received. Sure enough, a few months later I received a notice informing me it was time to renew and to remit $80. No yearly inspection is required in Florida. Just pay by mail and go on your merry way. I never thought I would miss the New York inspections, but after driving behind some of these vehicles in Florida, I would welcome that law to be enforced down here. I can't believe how many cars are on the road needing exhaust systems, new tires, windows, and so on. Trust me; there is air pollution in Florida.

After this not-so-enjoyable experience, we went to an insurance agency to purchase auto and homeowner's insurance policies. As expected, the car insurance was cheaper, but the homeowner's insurance was not. It can be cheaper if you don't want to include "sinkhole coverage." Sometimes, in Florida, the earth just collapses and brings down anything on its surface, including homes, buildings, and roads. This wonderful event is known as a "sinkhole." I had heard of sinkholes, but I never worried about them on Long Island. Besides, our Florida real estate agent was pretty adamant that we did not need this coverage, because we purchased in an area that does not have that risk. This appears to have been true, but according to the insurance agent, Florida homes do not have basements because of the high water level. After hearing all the pros and cons, I had come to the conclusion that Florida is a swamp no matter where you build, and I would rather be safe than sorry. As we continued going through the list of discounts available for a new home compliant with all the new building codes, the insurance agent asked if we had installed a power-surge protector. She informed us that we were in the lightning capital of the United States, and during the summer months, we would be experiencing daily thunderstorms with severe lightning. I looked at my husband and just wanted to explode. Let me see, in order to keep a promise, I had to put up with hot, humid weather most of the year, sinkholes, severe thunderstorms, possible tornados, and water that I could not drink and ruins our clothing. The power surge/energy saver would cost approximately $550. So far, I did not see much savings, but I was experiencing a lot of new concerns that I didn't need at that stage of my life. Yet I purchased the policies and convinced myself that it was too late to do anything else but continue with this temporary move.

On our way back to our rental, I was very down, when I received a call from my cousins. They would be vacationing in Florida for a week, arriving on May 27th and leaving June 2nd. This was good news. They could visit us at the rental and then see our new home. My thoughts were to immediately call the airlines and see if I could get a flight back home with them. So after speaking with them and getting their flight numbers, I dialed the airlines and was fortunate to book a seat on the same flight. Since my husband hated to fly, he would drive up to New York the same day, and we would meet at my son's home. Later we could return the car plates, pick up some of our belongings, UPS some of our packed items, and, unfortunately, head back to Florida.

The next few days we went back to the department stores to purchase appliances and other household items. Funny, when we first went to price these appliances everything was in stock. Now that we were actually purchasing, nothing would be delivered until June 17th. I explained that we were closing on May 25th, but all the salespeople could do was apologize for the inconvenience. Luckily, we could stay at our friend's house until June.

Chapter 15

CLOSING DAY

MAY 25TH FINALLY ARRIVED. THE closing was a new experience for me and my husband. When we closed on our home in New York it took hours. Lawyers were present and real estate agents sat by talking to the bankers, the lawyers, and prospective clients. Every *i* had to be dotted, and every *t* had to be crossed. There were papers and signatures galore. Not in Florida! There we sat, my husband, the woman doing the closing, and myself. As she greeted us, we went to a conference room, and she handed me two sheets of paper. I asked for our agent, the seller, a lawyer, or anyone else needed to be present. The answer was, "No, just us." All we had to do was show proof of our homeowner's insurance policy and give her the certified check for the house. We signed each sheet of closing papers, and that was that! Still, when I think of the purchase, it totally blows my mind. I couldn't believe we were done in twenty minutes. With the key in hand, we visited our new home. My husband was so happy, and I couldn't stop crying. He tried so hard to console me, but I just kept saying that materialistic items don't mean a thing to me. Family and friends are my happiness. We finally left after about a half hour, got something to eat, and went back to our rental. As he was calling our relatives and giving them the "good news," I started packing for my trip back home. Our family members and friends were just as devastated as I was. It was simply a big crying fest. They all wished us good luck and happiness but clearly thought we were insane for purchasing a home so soon. As much as I reassured them that the move was only temporary and a short investment, they all told me they hoped it wasn't a mistake.

Chapter 16

A WELCOME VISIT

MY COUSINS FINALLY ARRIVED, AND it was so great to see them. We had a wonderful time at our rental and showed them around. They simply fell in love with that community and couldn't understand why we had not purchased a home there. Apparently they were in agreement with my husband that the place had everything, and they loved the golf cart transportation. They liked the fact that all the stores, movie houses, church, eateries, gyms, golf courses, medical facilities, polo club, and entertainment were on the premises. The nightly music and dancing was also a plus for them. As we enjoyed the night together, we made arrangements to see our new home and community the next day.

After breakfast, we met with my cousins and drove to our new community. Before showing them the home, we escorted them around. They were amazed with the elegancy of the surroundings and the amenities. They immediately saw the differences between the two communities and could understand our decision. Once we came to our front door, they could see the better quality of the home itself. When we opened the door, their mouths remained open, and they said they could not believe how beautiful the whole place looked. I kept explaining that this was the model; therefore, everything was obviously perfect for each room. We stayed for awhile. My cousins tried so hard to reassure me that all would be fine once we moved in. They kept repeating that New York was only a couple hours away by plane, and, should we decide to make Florida our permanent residency, most of our family and friends have always said they too would like to retire to Florida. Somehow, this did not help. I just kept telling them I appreciated all their good wishes and compliments on the house; however, there is no place like home. Home to me is where my children and grandchildren reside. Home is where the heart is, as they say. Home is New York. "I will try to adapt," I said, "but if I can't, I will sell and go back where I belong." They advised my husband to enjoy Florida and the house while it lasted. It was the first time I really laughed since I arrived in Florida.

A few days later, my cousins and I drove to the airport to make our way back to New York. I was so happy. The flight was perfect, and it was good to see my son waiting for me at the airport. After a quick good-bye to my cousins, I hopped in my son's car, and we were off to Brooklyn. The ride to Brooklyn from Long Island was not very pleasant. As usual, the Long Island Expressway was packed with traffic. My son was very upset and could not understand why we bought a house so soon. He was disappointed with our decision, to say the least. I explained the situation regarding finances and how I promised to give it a try for Dad, but this did not satisfy him. I also told him about my prayers and answers and that now was the time to be in Florida—for what reason I, did not know. However, I also knew it would be temporary, and I would be back.

I understand my son, as he is much like I am in regard to family closeness. He and his wife enjoy that we are true grandparents. They want us to be involved in their children's lives and to make memories of holidays, special occasions, or just everyday life. I reassured him that this would still happen, just not now. It's true that we had this closeness to our grandchildren all our lives, and we would have it again. I explained that we would be back in New York for the holidays and try to fly home for special occasions. Somehow, to him, this was not the same, and I silently agreed.

We finally arrived at his home. My beautiful daughter-in-law and two precious granddaughters were sitting on the stoop waiting for us. It was so good to see them. Although only a month had passed, you would have thought it had been a year. We hugged and kissed, and life was good again. We had a great time during dinner, and it was nice to have the girls on my lap until bedtime. The next morning was even better when their grandpa rang the doorbell. Even though they were only one and two years of age at the time, the girls were so excited and jumped around when their grandpa appeared. We spent the whole day just playing with the kids and calling friends and relatives.

The following day we visited our daughter and three grandchildren. It was great to see them. Again the reception was over the top. My daughter's outlook regarding our move was different from my son's. She seemed to believe that Florida was not that far from New York and that we could still continue our close relationship. Her philosophy was that her dad deserved to be happy and that it was time for us to do whatever we want and enjoy our retirement. From her point of view, we could visit whenever we wanted, keep in contact by phone or computer messaging, and nothing would really change. In the event that it did not work out, we could always sell the house and move back to New York. I realized how different my two children were. You might think my daughter would be more sensitive and family-minded and my son would be more matter of fact. My grandmother used to say: "When it comes to children, look at your hand. You have five fingers, but all are different. Yet they resemble each other and have their special characteristics to make a beautiful hand. This is the same with children; all are different, with special talents to make a beautiful family."

During our visit, we continued seeing friends, relatives and arranging for our belongings to ship to our home on June 17th. Before I could blink, it was time to jam-pack our car with boxes and head back to Florida. I was as miserable and depressed to leave New York as I had been happy to arrive. These past six-weeks had been a roller coaster of emotions. I hoped I would calm myself once I was settled in the new house. When we finally arrived at our rental, we started packing our belongings. The next day we would be starting our new life in our Florida house.

Chapter 17

THE MOVE

O N JUNE 17, 2010, MY husband opened the door to our new home. I was carrying my grandmother's crucifix, a container of salt, and a bottle of holy water. This was a tradition of my family. The crucifix represents bringing God into our home, the salt represents the salt of the earth and is to provide for our needs, and the holy water is for the house to be truly blessed. After my husband hung the crucifix in our bedroom, I blessed each room with the holy water and placed the salt in our pantry.

Unpacking the car kept us busy as we awaited our appliances' delivery. The washer, dryer, and TV arrived in perfect condition. However, the refrigerator, which my husband and I argued over before purchasing, was too large for the kitchen. After saying, "I told you so," at least ten times, I called the store to order the refrigerator I had wanted originally. I told the delivery men that they could come back the following day with the new fridge and to please take back the refrigerator that Mr. Wonderful insisted on.

As this fiasco went on, UPS arrived with our ten boxes from New York. They had cost approximately $600 to ship. Half of the boxes, all of which had "FRAGILE" written on them in very large letters, were crushed as if an elephant had sat on them. Of course, the UPS guy wouldn't stay as I opened these packages and advised me to call them if there were any damages. A five-year-old could have seen there was plenty of damage. I began to open the boxes, and, sure enough, all my crystal stemware, which I had since my engagement party and bridal shower in 1968, was smashed to bits. Many glass mementos from my mother and grandmother were also destroyed. Collectibles that I had accumulated over the years were unsalvageable.

As I tried to compose myself, I called UPS. They were very sorry for the breakage and advised me that, since I had insured all these items, I should keep them in the original boxes with their wrappings. A UPS man could come pick them up and have the boxes inspected. I followed their instructions to a tee. However, these items had sentimental value, more than cash value, and this thought left me empty. After dozens of calls to UPS over a span of three weeks, I finally got a check for $100 for one box. I called and explained five boxes were damaged. According to UPS, I didn't pack them properly. I found this hard to believe. I had packed the items from Long Island to Maine, from Maine back to Long Island, from Long Island to Iceland, from Iceland back to Long Island, and several other moves over the years without a chip on anything, and all of a sudden I don't know how to pack? As people say, "You can't fight city hall."

Our refrigerator finally arrived, and it was time to go food shopping. For the past six weeks we had eaten out, picked up items at local stores, and never went to the supermarket. The supermarkets in Florida are beautiful, clean, and have the friendliest workers. However, the prices are outrageous. As I entered the store, I was welcomed by a greeter. "How y'all doin'?" he said with a beautiful smile. I replied, "Fine, thank you." I went to the produce section and couldn't understand why all the items were double the cost that I normally paid in New York. Wasn't Florida supposedly cheaper? Most of the items I was purchasing were grown in Florida. I had seen farms all over the place. What was driving the prices so high? As I went down the cereal aisle, an employee asked, "How y'all doin'?" I replied, "Fine, thank you." I looked at cereal that I normally pay five dollars for two boxes in New York, here they were priced twice that. Next aisle another employee asked, "How y'all doin'?"

Okay, this is getting ridiculous, I thought. I just wasn't used to this. In New York, a customer was lucky to find an employee willing to help her when she really needed it! Normally, I would complain about that, but at least I was in and out of the store in no time. If this kept up, I would be spending double the money I normally spend on groceries and I would be in the store an extra half hour just talking to employees! I tried to stay civil while I visited the meat counter. Would you believe every piece of meat was a dollar or two per pound higher than in New York? This was nuts! There were farms with plenty of cows, pigs, and chickens located only a few miles from my new neighborhood. What gives? By the time I was walking down the fifth aisle and meeting the fifth employee who wanted to know how I was doing, I wanted to get a megaphone and yell, "I am truly miserable and don't want to be here or pay these crazy prices. I refuse to pay five dollars for a box of cereal, ninety-nine cents per pepper, a dollar for a sad-looking orange, and I want to go home!" However, I managed to make it to the cashier, who was also interested in my state of being. Finally another employee insisted on bagging and carrying my goods to my car. I gave my husband the "wife look." He looked back at me and just smiled. He really found the experience quite refreshing. He loved how the employees were so nice and even wanted to bring our groceries to the car. Honestly, I understand that this is the way it should be, but after so many years in the rat race, I prefer to do it my way, get my stuff at cheap prices, and get the hell out of the store with as little conversation as possible. I prefer running up and down the aisles and not creeping along trying to avoid bumping into people who are either in a wheelchair or motorized shopping cart. I realize this sounds harsh. But it truly takes time to get used to the slower pace, and I just wasn't ready.

By the time we got our groceries home, the meats were totally defrosted. I had to cook most of the food. I realized then why so many people had coolers in their carts. Trust me, if you grocery shop in Florida during the months between May and October, bring an insulated shopping bag or a cooler. If you don't, prepare to cook as soon as you unpack the items.

The shopping was now done, and I had cooked our very expensive dinner. I wondered why my steak was so tough and the side dishes didn't taste the same. I have since learned that the meat is not the same quality that we get in New York because of the way they feed the cattle in Florida. I have also realized that the wonderful-tasting water in Florida can make your cooking taste a little different. Oh, I was loving Florida more and more.

Chapter 18

TRY TO THINK POSITIVE

I*T'S A NEW DAY. LET'S try and have some optimistic feelings. We'll have a nice breakfast and go shopping for some summer clothes.* When we purchased the house we were told a shopping mall was only fifteen minutes away. Trying to put a smile on my face, we went to the gas station and happily noted gas was about twenty cents cheaper than back home. Then we drove to the so-called mall. It sure was taking us longer than fifteen minutes. *Maybe it's just down the road,* we kept saying. We finally arrived. It actually took about twenty-five minutes to get there because of the forty-five-mile-an-hour zones, slow drivers, and mostly one-lane roads. Most of the stores were out of business due to the bad economy, the food court was under a tent that the sun was beating down on, and the stores that were open did not have much to choose from. This definitely was not a place many people shopped. So we got back in our car, planning to go home and then try another mall about twenty-five minutes away. We were about to leave when the sky opened with lightning and thunder you could not imagine. It seems June through November is the storm season. Of course, I knew this but didn't realize it would happen on a daily basis. I thought we might experience a storm now and then. Nope, every day like clockwork it would rain heavily, lightning, and thunder. Florida would have been the perfect location for Dr. Frankenstein's lab. The winds were another story. All I can say is an umbrella is of no use. Just grin and bear it. Get accustomed to the fact you are going to get drenched. It's really okay, because before you know it, you'll be nice and dry in no time. As I tell everyone: We have tropical weather. We have tropical insects. We have tropical animals. Hello, we are in the tropics! Of course, all the snowbirds love it down here January through April, but that's because they do not experience real Florida living.

It took us over thirty minutes to reach our house. However, in that time, the weather changed from thunderstorm to a hot and muggy ninety-five degrees. I simply could not breathe. After a short stay indoors, I agreed to continue with our plans and venture to the other mall, supposedly only a twenty-five-minute drive away. Forget about that! It took over forty minutes. However, it was much nicer than the previous mall. At least there were some familiar stores, and it was totally modern and air conditioned. I won't go into detail about the crazy entrance and exits of the parking lots. It seems no common sense was used when planning them. I will tell you, I am not the only person who feels this way. Everyone I have met agrees with my opinion. Even Mr. Wonderful admits this to be true. At least the trip wasn't a total waste of time. We managed to pick up the clothes we needed at slightly higher prices, and Mr. Wonderful found golf balls on sale. What a great day! Somehow, the savings on gas cost us more time and money in travelling to shops that were more costly than New York. I was not happy. But it was only the second day; I had to give it time.

By the third day, clothing and food were accounted for. The house was immaculate, and I had nothing to do. My husband, on the other hand, was ready to play *free golf*. (Of course there really is no free golf in Florida. You still have to pay for cart fees.) I figured this would be a good time to cook a nice meal, make a few phone calls, and simply watch television while he enjoyed the sun and the golf game. *Let's take the pressure off and just try to relax*, I told myself. As he left, with a big smile on his face, I was just as happy to do my own thing. All the togetherness we had had recently was driving me crazy! Back home, the children, grandchildren, and family events broke up the week and the "togetherness." My card games at the condo, volunteer work at the church, and condo board duties also used to keep me quite busy. I had a life!

After four weeks of getting up in the morning, seeing the sun, having breakfast, trying to keep myself occupied while my husband went golfing, I started to feel like Bill Murray in the movie *Groundhog Day*. It hit me that I was becoming a golf widow. Depression was setting in, and as I asked God to show me the reason for my being in Florida, my doorbell rang. Wiping the tears from my eyes, I opened the door. There stood a lady in every sense of the word. She appeared to be very apprehensive as she introduced herself. Her name was Mary Jo, and she had just moved into her new home across the street. She informed me that our sales agent had told her to look me up. Our agent felt that we would get along just fine because we had so much in common.

As I invited her in, I remembered that our agent had spoken of Mary Jo and hoped I would introduce myself to her. To be truthful, I had no intentions of doing so. That's just the way I am. As forward as I am, I never initiate a friendship.

As we both smiled and sat at my kitchen table, we began speaking of our backgrounds. As she spoke so softly and intellectually, I had this feeling I was speaking to a former nun. She continued to explain how she moved to Florida from Indiana so that she could be with her daughter and granddaughter, who lived close to our community. She was a widow, and her son lived in Oregon. Her eldest daughter still resided in Indiana. I also spoke of my children and background. It's funny, but somehow a farm girl from Indiana and a city kid from Brooklyn were clicking. We were speaking just a few minutes when we realized we were actually conversing like we knew each other for years. Our ideologies about life, religion, rearing children, and other subjects were so identical. It was really uncanny. The only big difference we had was on politics. Yet we felt the same about what was right and what was unfair about politicians. We simply had different views on how to correct the wrongs and how to make the world a better place. We laughed over how our votes would cancel each other. We immediately felt a connection. When she was leaving, she wondered aloud if I would like to join her at water aerobics and then shopping the following day. I accepted. We have talked or seen each other practically every day for the past two years.

When my husband came home from golf, I told him about May Jo. He was happy to learn of the woman who put a smile on my face. I also told him that, as much as I liked her and enjoyed her company, I had a feeling she was a nun at one time, and the only thing that could screw this friendship up was my foul language. I am not proud of having a profanity problem. However, when I am angry or flustered the f-word flies. Somehow I find this word so appropriate and versatile in many situations. It's amazing. I can control my tongue when I am around my children or grandchildren, but when I am just being myself, I turn into a truck driver.

The next day when I saw Mary Jo, we had a great time swimming, getting a bite to eat, and shopping. Finally, I told her my inner thoughts. I explained about my use of profanity and that I knew it would show its ugly head sooner or later. I also explained my feeling that she was once a nun. She was so genuine about the situation and assured me that she would not take offense to my bad language. You see, she was a nun for nine years and was also a retired high school and college teacher. During her teaching years, she had heard a lot. I was so relieved. The next couple of weeks of friendship were passed by mainly speaking of our childhood and family history. She told me of the longevity in her family. Her grandfather fought in the Civil War, and her mother lived for over ninety years. Unfortunately, I do not have longevity in my family. My mom died a week after her sixty-sixth birthday, and my dad passed away at age seventy-one. At the end of this conversation, she said that the reason we both moved to Florida was to meet each other and that I must be the one to take care of her when her time came. I looked at her and explained that I had no intention of staying in Florida until she was well in her nineties. As a matter of fact, I was putting the house up for sale after the holidays. She was very distraught that I wanted to return to New York. She also hoped I would change my mind.

Mary Jo and I did many things together these past two years. We really enjoyed each other by just chatting, going to lunch, shopping, gambling at the local casino, travelling to New Orleans, attending Mass, and going to church functions. My husband and I have been very grateful to her, and we have become a real threesome. Sure, we went to restaurants and social events, but we were also there for each other at doctor's appointments, hospital stays, and unhappy circumstances in both of our lives. Our fun and honest relationship was going just great until March 2012 when Mary Jo was diagnosed with cancer and given only six months to live. As I am writing this chapter, her daughter Clare and I are taking care of her. Who would have thought two years ago that an innocent speculation would actually come true? Needless to say, I have taken my home off the market until either a miracle occurs or Mary Jo goes back home to Our Father in Heaven. (See postscript.)

Chapter 19

NEW BEGINNINGS

MY HUSBAND BEGAN TO REALLY make a new life in Florida. After only two months in our new home, he joined the Knights of Columbus and the Moose Club. As he dragged me to their functions, I met very nice people, but I didn't want to get actively involved. This was a total turn-a-round for us. Back home I was in the Columbiettes and joined many groups, while my husband refused to join anything. Now all of a sudden he was the social butterfly, and I simply had no interest.

Luckily, we attended Mass every Sunday, but our new church was hard to get used to. Somehow it had a southern flare to it. (DUH!) It was humbling to see so many elderly people at Mass. My husband and I were two of the youngest, at age sixty-one. Very few families with children attended Mass. The hymns were the same, but they had a lively kick. There were also a lot of "amens" from the priest and the congregation during the homily. I have since gotten comfortable with this, but I can't help missing the way we participated at Mass back home in New York.

I was fortunate to meet my friend, Dolores, at Mass. My husband and I happened to sit next to her one Sunday. When it came time to shake hands and give each other the sign of peace, she asked me if I was from New York. Of course there was no denying it. It seems I have a New York accent. She also came from New York, Astoria specifically. After Mass we conversed and exchanged telephone numbers. From that day on, we have been close friends. She introduced me to several women, and we all have a great time shopping, going to yard sales, eating out, and just being together. I must say, as much as I want to go back home, I would miss these wonderful women, who have helped keep me sane.

Chapter 20

MEDICAL EXPERIENCES

I N JULY AND AUGUST 2010, my husband was not feeling well. We went to several doctors and emergency visits to the hospital. I believed he had a gall bladder problem. However, all tests revealed that his gall bladder was functioning normally. This problem persisted until January 2012. For a year and a half, he saw doctors and specialists every month, plus had several hospital stays. In New York, the insurance we had was affordable, and we never had a problem. Unfortunately, this type of insurance was not available in Florida, so we needed to switch. The co-pays of our first new policy were quite a bit higher, and many doctors did not accept the insurance. So we switched again to another insurance company. This insurance was more costly but allowed us to visit more doctors. Once again, Florida was costing us more. I can't complain about all the specialists my husband was referred to, as they were very thorough. But I do feel many office visits, exams and medications he was given during this time were a total waste. I can't say for sure our New York doctors would have found a solution to his problem more quickly, but I really wonder. After seeing several specialists, my original diagnosis was correct. He had a benign tumor in his gall bladder that was attached to his liver. His gall bladder was removed in January 2012. Thankfully, he is currently doing fine. This was an eye-opening experience, and it made us realize the differences in medical care from state to state. The hospitals and doctors in Florida are wonderful, but we are more comfortable with our insurance and medical care back home.

Chapter 21

TRUDGING ALONG

I T WAS A LONG, HOT summer in 2010. Everyone we met informed us that the weather during this time of year was, of course, hot, but 2010 broke records. From June until December of that year, my husband and friends would literally drop me off at the front door of a store and pick me up at that same door. I simply could not breathe in such hot, humid weather. On Thanksgiving Day, the temperature was over ninety degrees. There I was, cooking a turkey with all the trimmings for two people and feeling like it was the Fourth of July and I should be having a barbeque. I still feel as if I am in *The Twilight Zone* when it comes to holidays in Florida. I shop for Christmas gifts in capri slacks and sandals while listening to songs with lyrics like, "Baby it's cold outside," "Let it snow," and "Chestnuts roasting on an open fire." Meanwhile the sun is shining, and temperatures are in the high seventies. In the winter, the locals dress as if it were forty degrees outside. Some elderly people wear scarves, jackets, winter slacks, and even gloves when the temperature is about sixty degrees. Stores have the usual Christmas sales, including discounts on boots! Who the heck needs boots in that weather? Are you kidding me? This all goes on while the store Santa waits for kids to sit on his lap. The poor man is sweating to death in his Santa suit with the fan blowing directly on him and his beard flying in the breeze. It's a sight to behold. Amidst this scene are very cheerful salespeople and patrons singing along with the piped Christmas songs. There are Christmas decorations galore. Yet a lighted snowflake, Santa, or Noel candle just doesn't make me feel festive, as it glistens in the sun and is attached to a palm tree.

I have also found huge differences in holiday shopping from what I am used to. In Florida, chestnuts are hard to find, there are no crowds or long lines at the checkout counter, and I am the only one with a full cart of groceries or gifts! It seems the people down here keep life as simple as possible. They would rather eat out and give gift cards. They have explained to me that it is cheaper to go with the early-bird specials or to dine with their friends at their club affiliation. I've started to think they have the right idea. It is quite depressing eating a Thanksgiving dinner for two. All the grocery shopping, cost, and preparation are really not worth it. Even though my husband and I try to keep the holiday spirit, all the food in the world could not replace the family we are missing. Eating Thanksgiving leftovers for a week is also a downer.

I prefer the cold, crisp air of November and December back home. I need the maddening crowds and the family. The only bright side of getting over the Thanksgiving Day letdown is that, in a couple of weeks, we are closer to being back in New York to celebrate Christmas and New Year's Day with our children and grandchildren.

Chapter 22

CHRISTMAS 2010

W E WERE ON OUR WAY! The car was fully packed with gifts and suitcases. The weather in Florida was perfect for travelling, and both of us were anxious to get to Brooklyn.

What a great trip we were having. Christmas was the best ever. Hugs and kisses were plentiful. Laughing with the little ones was a great treat. Going to Mass on a cold day and seeing all the Christmas decorations in church was beautiful and appropriate. Everything was going just perfectly, when we got the worst snowstorm ever. My husband was finally coming around to realizing all we have given up to move to Florida. Then the snow started falling and continued for days. We were stuck in my son's apartment for five days. My husband shoveled snow each day. Mayor Bloomberg only had certain streets plowed, and, unfortunately, my son's block was not one of them. I had no problem with looking out the living room window to watch the snow accumulate, the neighbors cursing the snow, and drivers yelling at each other and flipping the finger. I found it quite normal and amusing. However, my husband was tired of shoveling, hated the snow, and couldn't wait for the plow to remove all the white stuff so we could go back to the Sunshine State. His wish was finally granted, and a few days later, we began making our way back to Florida.

Chapter 23

BACK TO ABNORMAL

H APPY NEW YEAR 2011! WE were back to the usual everyday life in Florida, with my husband either golfing or visiting doctors and me back with my friends shopping, going to yard sales, and eating out. This may seem like heaven to some, but for me it was not living. After months of discussions about moving back to New York and missing my granddaughter's birthday in March, my husband was starting to understand my needs.

He truly grasped my loneliness when it was time to celebrate his birthday in April. As he received numerous cards from family and friends, I noticed he was getting a little teary eyed. As I sang, "Happy birthday to you," with no one else around, he agreed this day was not too happy. However, the icing on the cake was when UPS arrived with a beautiful fruit arrangement from our niece, Maria. She sent a note that really touched him. Maria is like a daughter to us, and she calls us her second mom and dad. We love each other to pieces. Her note was so loving, it brought my husband to tears, and he admitted it was time to go back home. He immediately put up the "For Sale" sign, which I had bought months ago, on our lawn. I guess it was just too much for him to see how our children, grandchildren, and niece kept missing and loving him. They all wanted him back home where he belonged. When he placed that sign on our front lawn, I was so happy. You know what, he was happy too.

We have had many lookers and two real buyers since that day. Unfortunately, the two buyers who were in contract on their homes never actually sold their homes, because their buyers could not get mortgages. We still have their names, but they still can't close the deal on their houses. In the past year, we have had more lookers than buyers. Many of them come from New York, all with the same story of trying to sell their home and being eager to get away from the high cost of living and the snow. They all love our home. The house really sells itself. However, it seems the husbands who come are ready to retire and make a new life, while the wives are not really sold on Florida or leaving their children and grandchildren. I have found this to be true with the majority of people I have met in Florida.

Chapter 24

INSECTS, REPTILES, AND BEARS—OH MY!

IN THE MONTH OF MAY 2011, I got a pleasant Mother's Day surprise from my daughter and granddaughter. I couldn't imagine who was ringing my doorbell that day. It was just wonderful. However, during their stay they told me that my son-in-law's workplace was relocating to Georgia, and they wanted me to accompany them to Georgia to meet with a real estate agent who would show them some houses to rent. Of course I agreed, but it seemed so untimely. We had just put the "For Sale" sign on our property in order to be with them in New York, and now they might be moving to Georgia! I realize you cannot live your life around your children, but this was a twist that I never saw coming.

On our way to Georgia, we started to see swarms of flying insects. I mean, the windshield was completely covered. I remembered these nasty bugs from the previous September, but I hadn't seen them since then. My daughter and granddaughter couldn't believe it. I explained that the insects were called "love bugs." They infest the area during the months of May and September. They continuously mate for awhile and then drop dead, leaving their eggs in the ground somewhere until it's time for the new generation to rise up, mate, and die. I explained that this was the story I got from the residents, and, so far, it appeared to be true. My daughter and granddaughter were disgusted, just as I was. "But," I told them, "If you think this is disgusting, take a good look at the motorcyclists' helmets and clothing when they stop at a red light. They are all covered with these bugs." Gross, but true.

Before long, we stopped for gas and saw a black snake. I explained this was a common sight. That's why I didn't walk to my mail box or anyplace. Everyone told me the black snake is a good snake that eats rodents and the bad snakes. Personally, I don't want to get near any snake to find out if it's a good one or bad one. Naturally, they were curious about the alligators. I explained that we didn't have to worry about them because I did not live near any water areas. Although, our place was located on the west coast and had plenty of natural wildlife, our community was twelve miles away from the Gulf of Mexico.

I did warn them about the nasty red ants. Those little buggers can bite the heck out of you. They are just as bad as the no-see-ums, a bug that you really can't see but will surely feel when they bite. Scorpions and small venomous spiders are also around. I explained that I had an exterminator contract not only for termites but for all the wonderful creepy crawlers. Thank God, I haven't had a problem. I haven't seen anything in the house, not even a nasty roach, by which I am terrified. I explained to them to get ready for the change of weather, wildlife, and little creatures in the South; after all, the area of Georgia that they were relocating to was not much different from the northwest coast of Florida. The funny part of this conversation came when we saw a sign that said, "Beware of bear crossing." I just shrugged my shoulders and told them that, so far, I hadn't seen any.

After all was said and done, my daughter and her family moved to Georgia in August 2011. This was one month after my son moved to Long Island, only six blocks away from the house my daughter just left! *I give up!*

Chapter 25

MISSING THE LITTLE THINGS

As much as Florida has to offer, this spoiled New Yorker never realized how she would miss the everyday life of New York.

When I was growing up in Brooklyn, everything I needed was in walking distance. If I wanted to go to the beach or the city, all I had to do was hop on a train. Moving to Long Island still afforded me the same lifestyle; everything took only minutes to get to by car.

I could find a New York—style pizza, bagel, or deli. Italian bakeries, German bakeries, Greek diners, ethnic specialty groceries, and restaurants were everywhere. Can you tell I like to eat? It must be my Italian heritage. Florida has all these foods and places, but nothing tastes the same. Many establishments claim to be New York—style this and New York—style that, but they don't even come close. Everyone faults the water. If I were a proprietor in Florida, I would purchase my water from New York, make delicious food, and charge a bit more. There are so many people who have moved from New York, New

Jersey, Connecticut, and Massachusetts that would patronize their establishment.

Never in a million years did I think I'd miss New York's local news and weather channels. I always thought our newspapers left a lot to be desired. But in Florida, I don't know why I even watch the news and weather. Every day is practically the same. The news shows feature a car crash, a domestic killing, a sexual offender, two local politicians (one for Obama's policies, the other contradicting his views), and the same weather pattern for weeks at a time.

The local weatherman should just tape his predictions. He could have one tape from January to March forecasting sun and temperatures in the seventies, with a possible cold front of sixty degrees in the morning. April to May would be sunny with temperatures warming to the high eighties. June through October would be hot and humid, with temperatures reaching the nineties and possible thunderstorms or tornadoes and a hurricane watch for most areas. November and December would always be beautiful, with temperatures starting in the sixties and reaching the seventies. I'm serious: give or take a few exceptions, you have just read the local weather for an entire year. I truly miss a daily forecast of different weather conditions. I don't mind a rainy forecast one day, snow another day, and warm temperatures the next day. It makes me feel like each day is new.

I try reading the local newspaper. It simply repeats the previously mentioned news and weather conditions. Its advertisements for the local stores and supermarkets could be photocopied from previous editions. Every other week, the same stores have the same items on sale. So one week I go to one chain outlet and grocery store to pick up their sales items. The next week I switch to the other chain outlet and grocery store to pick up their sales items. I simply pay the same price all month long. It's so monotonous. The only new news in the newspaper is the obituary column. It is more uplifting than the New York obituaries. The majority of people passing away live until their late eighties or nineties. Quite a few of them make it to one hundred years old. I must tell you, as much as they loved Florida, most of them take a last flight home to be buried in the state of their birth.

I never thought I would miss visiting New York City. For years, I only went to the City once in a while to see a show. I would think of going more often, but always put it off. I kept telling myself, *I'll go another time to see the Christmas show at Radio City. I'll attend the next lighting of the city Christmas tree. Maybe next year I'll revisit Ellis Island, the Statue of Liberty, and all the wonderful places the City has to offer.* Now that I live in Florida and watch all the New York events, such as the St. Patrick's Day Parade, New Year's Eve at Times Square, and Macy's Fourth of July Firework Show, I see how I took all these happenings for granted.

Would you believe I miss young ones acting up in church or in a restaurant? Honestly, wherever I go, "I see old people." When I am with the young, it makes me feel alive. When I dine out, I am surrounded by the elderly. This makes me feel like I am in a nursing home. When I attend Mass, the majority of the people will not shake hands to give the sign of peace. They just nod. I found out they fear catching germs and getting sick. They all have their set seats and groups of friends. Therefore, they refuse to move, and you must climb over them to the middle of the pew. Instead of hearing parents whispering to their children, you hear every conversation loud and clear regarding their doctors' appointments, their operations, and who passed away.

I long for a shopping area that has more than CVS, Walgreen's, and Wal-Mart. I laugh at the pharmacies' outdoor advertisements, for example, "Free Breast Pump Rentals." *Seriously?* Since I moved to Florida, I think I have seen approximately a dozen pregnant women.

The rest of the women have been in menopause for decades. Besides, who would rent a breast pump?

I have always enjoyed handing out candy for Halloween. Seeing the parents and children walking up and down the streets in costume was the treat for me. I would make at least a hundred bags of goodies for the little ones and always kept a spare bag of candy, just in case I ran out. I have spent two Halloweens in Florida, and not a single child has shown up. I ride around the neighborhood and see plenty of decorations on the doors and windows, but they seem out of place with the sun shining until eight o'clock at night and the temperatures in the eighties. Maybe the temperatures have a lot to do with it. Children would be sweating, and all their make-up would simply melt down their faces. There are schools all around me. So where are the kids?

I really enjoyed our fenced backyard in New York. It's true it costs more to have a plot on a golf course in Florida. You not only have a beautiful view, but it affords you more privacy. This is the sales pitch. Somehow, I do not find it so prestigious. Yes, it's nice to have an open view with no neighbors in the back of your home. However, from eight in the morning until seven in the evening, you will see a variety of sights. There are the early golfers who prefer to walk the course. These are typically older gentlemen. They wear outfits you would not believe and are sweating profusely, dragging their clubs, and waving respectfully to me as I sit on my lanai. Unfortunately, most of them have a hearing problem, which causes them to speak very loudly. They can never find their golf ball due either to poor vision or their egos, which make them look for their golf balls much farther from where they actually hit them. So every morning I try to direct them to their misplaced golf balls. I really don't mind. At least I get to speak to someone and feel I am helping them save time from being in the heat. After they go on their merry way, a few groups of ladies start driving by in their golf carts. They usually play in a foursome. Some wear such colorful outfits and look so professional that you would think they knew how to play a decent game. However, the majority just look good. Personally, I think they should be playing croquet. The last groups are the men in their sixties who still think they can play like Tiger Woods. I admit that they hit the golf ball farther than the first two groups, but they too have their problems. Although their outfits are not as outlandish as the earlier golfers, they also suffer from hearing loss. They always over compensate their swing to the right or left, and they too believe they hit the ball farther than they actually have. I have no pity for these gentlemen and never direct them to their lost golf balls. I've tried in the past, but they totally ignore me. Somehow, I miss my little backyard with our barbeque and lawn chairs that I can actually keep on my lawn and my backyard neighbors.

I could go on and on about how I didn't stop to smell the roses while I lived in New York. However, I think I've made my point.

Chapter 26

TO MOVE OR NOT TO MOVE

THE YEAR 2011 WAS THE same as 2010. Every day just ran into the next. Of course, we made a few trips to New York, which helped the year pass. One special time during that year was when Mary Jo and I took a trip to New Orleans in September. I was feeling very depressed. It was my birthday, and the phone calls I received were just not the same as having everyone at the house to celebrate. Usually when I start feeling this way, I pack my bags and go on a trip. Over the course of my marriage, it was common for my husband to come home from work and find a note from me stating I went to Atlantic City, Foxwoods, or Mohegan Sun. There were times I informed him that I had just made reservations and booked a flight to Biloxi, Las Vegas, or to Georgia to visit friends. A real shocker for him was when I took a trip to Fatima, in Portugal, and Lourdes, France, for two weeks. I have no problem travelling by myself, especially since he hates to fly and doesn't really care for travel. So sitting alone on my birthday, I decided to book a five-day bus trip from Florida to New Orleans. I no sooner confirmed my reservation when Mary Jo rang my doorbell to wish me a happy birthday. I told her of my plans, and she shook her head in disbelief. She would never take such a spontaneous trip and without discussing the matter with her husband. Then she told me of how much she had enjoyed New Orleans and how it was one of the last vacations she had with her late husband, Max. She meekly asked if I would mind if she accompanied me on my trip. Of course, before the words were out of her mouth, I called the agency and made plans for the two of us. She was as excited as a kid on Christmas morning. The next day, Dolores called asking what I had been doing. I told her that Mary Jo and I had just made plans to visit New Orleans in October. Once I told her the details, she called our other friend Sheila, and before I knew it, the four of us were on our way. My husband drove all of us to the bus, and we all had a great five days. So much for my spontaneous ideas!

October and November flew by, and soon my husband and I were back in the car driving home for Christmas. We stayed with my son for the holidays. My daughter and her family also visited. Being with family was just wonderful. The weather was absolutely great. We were all hoping the New Year would bring a buyer to our home and we could resume our lives back in New York.

The main reason I wrote this book was to help people decide if they really want to leave their home and start a "new life" in a different state. You must want to begin this new life and look at it as a new chapter. If you can't do that, then you should be a snowbird. I suggest you rent a place for at least six months to a year before purchasing a home. "Sales of the century" are always available. In the South, people are always selling their homes at low prices. You can bargain for a new home all the time, whether by lowering the price or by adding upgrades. Foreclosures and short sales are plentiful. Don't be tricked by salespeople giving you the impression that, if you don't buy "right now," you will be missing out on the greatest deal ever.

When you rent or vacation in Florida with the intent to eventually move, do not go into vacation mode. Money goes quickly when you feel like you are on a vacation, rather than a test run of day-to-day living. If moving to Florida, truly get to know the state by visiting the northern, central and southern parts. It's a large state with diversified weather conditions, people, and special areas for special interests. If you prefer three seasons, what I consider hot, hotter, and hottest, stay north. You must decide if you prefer the west coast to the east coast. The coasts have different types of beaches, wildlife, and weather. You may prefer the southern part of Florida if you really enjoy very hot weather and tropical conditions all year long. Central Florida has a lot to offer, but it is obviously not for beachgoers. Research the areas carefully; like any place else there are good areas and not so good areas. There are heavily populated cities, which have a faster pace of life with more stores, entertainment, and restaurants closer to your home. Conversely, there are many farm areas that afford you to have livestock and horses. Most areas appear to be for retired people: very quiet, with hardly any young people in the neighborhood and with golf courses, many amenities, and fewer stores in the vicinity. Our community happens to fall into the latter category, which is simply not my style. Even though a community might be family oriented and with lots of amenities to keep a person busy, make sure you are physically able to enjoy them. Also, if you are like me, you may get bored with playing cards, sitting by the pool, or other activities they offer.

A very important skill to learn is shopping as if you are living in Florida. Get to know the stores, the prices, and the travel times. Don't make the mistake I did by just going to the local stores for everyday items.

Consider your health insurance and doctors. It's important in the retirement stage of life. Don't think of Florida as God's waiting room. Too many people move to Florida with the idea that they are going to relax in the sun, golf, fish, and do whatever else they want to do before they die. Many people make Florida part of their "bucket list." Florida should not be like the mythical elephant graveyards, whereby an elephant gets old, leaves his herd, finds a place with other old elephants and just hangs around until it expires.

Florida is just like any other state when you become old. You enjoy life to its fullest, and then unfortunately the time comes when you must see a doctor or have a stay in the hospital. There are plenty of doctors and health-care facilities in Florida. However, it really is rough when you have to depend on neighbors to assist you in illness, whether the illness is curable or incurable. I would rather have a doctor who has known me for years and my family around for emotional support.

Always keep in mind that the money you will be saving on home owner's insurance, car insurance, utilities, and taxes can and will be spent on travelling expense, whether it be locally or back to your home state. Other items such as water, clothing, food, and so forth will be more expensive. Like everywhere else, what you save on one hand is spent with the other.

Realize, as much as relatives and friends say that they will visit you, life happens, and the visits will not be as often as you all had anticipated. Most important, if you are the type of person that believes home is where the heart is and you enjoy living close to your children, grandchildren, and friends, think three times before leaving them.

To end on a happier note, if you love the sun, golf, fishing, and a slow pace of life: Go for it! I have met many couples who have a lot in common and really love retirement in Florida. For these couples, it was both the husbands' and the wives' dreams to retire in Florida. That's the key: both must really want it. They not only enjoy being with each other, they truly enjoy everything about Florida. As much as I complain, I must admit Florida has a lot to offer for many people. A lot of couples are quite content to see their families twice a year. They realize, as they age, their trips up north may end, and it will be their children's turn to visit them. It doesn't matter to them, because they have made a wonderful life for themselves in Florida. There are so many church groups, senior citizen centers, and senior travel groups in Florida. If you and your spouse are golfers, enjoy outdoor sports, and like to socialize, then both of you will have plenty to do.

So many people do not miss the hustle and bustle of the city. They are content with local shows rather than Broadway. They don't care about food costs or going to real New York—style diners, pizza places, or delis; the early-bird specials are just super for them. It doesn't matter if the clothing or general items are priced higher, because they don't need much anymore.

Their grandchildren are grown and have their own lives, so there's no more missing recitals, plays, sleepovers, sporting events, or special occasions. I am truly happy for these people. God bless them! My hope is that they enjoy retirement in Florida for a long, long time. It must be nice! I hope you are one of those happy people and not a spoiled New Yorker like me. After forty-four years of marriage, I am grateful to have Mr. Wonderful, who is willing to move back to New York. If we are lucky enough to sell our home, I promised him he can return to Florida to vacation any time he chooses, and I won't complain! Now that's a compromise!

POSTSCRIPT

I am grateful to Mary Jo, who urged me to write this book. After many conversations during our first year of friendship, she would always say, "Rosemarie, you should write a book." I would explain that it was easy for her to say; she had degrees in English and German. She was a high school and college teacher with a strong academic background. I'm just a high school graduate that immediately went to work in the office world. I managed to climb the ladder from Dictaphone operator to private secretary, bookkeeper, assistant accountant, and, finally, office manager/administrative assistant. Although I had always wanted to attend college and become an accountant, the timing was never right, being a full-time mother and office worker. My comments infuriated her because she felt I was always putting myself down and didn't give myself credit for my work experience. In her eyes, I was her peer, not her subordinate. In order to make her happy, I told her I would try to write the book if she promised to proofread it. After she read it, edited it, and made sure I wasn't making a fool of myself, we would try to publish it. She agreed.

I started writings in February 2012. As mentioned, in March 2012, Mary Jo became ill and went back to Indiana to seek a cancer specialist and proper treatment. As she received these treatments, we would talk on the phone almost daily. I informed her that I was writing the book and told her she had better come back to Florida if she ever wanted to see the project completed. She wanted to be in Florida again with her daughter and granddaughter.

Unfortunately, on June 10th, she received the news that the cancer was spreading. She had a choice of trying a new form of treatment that would probably give her six months more to live or end treatment with likely only three more months of life. She called me and asked if I would be her caregiver, along with her daughter Clare, until it was her time. Of course, I agreed.

On June 18th, my husband and I picked up Mary Jo at Tampa Bay Airport. From that day, her daughter and I took forty-eight-hour shifts along with a hospice nurse who visited a couple of times a week. Due to Mary Jo's aggressive cancer, Clare and I decided to hire the hospice nurse for days and nights as of August 1st. Of course, we still visited Mary Jo for hours during the day. During this time, I continued to write. Finally, on August 6th, the book was complete. Mary Jo was fading quickly and slept most of the day. When I went to visit, I brought my draft. The hospice nurse informed me that Mary Jo was sleeping, but as soon as she heard my voice, Mary Jo called me to her bedroom. Her voice was so weak, and her eyes were half closed. Yet she wanted to visit. She inquired as to what I was holding. I explained that the book was complete. I kept my part of the bargain. She smiled and insisted that I read it to her. I told her I would just read a few pages and then she must rest. As I read, she laughed and smiled. Every few pages, I would urge her to close her eyes and rest. She would not do so until I finished the whole book. The nurse and I were simply amazed. She clapped her hands and whispered, "I told you that you could do it. I love your book, and I love you. Thank you."

I jokingly replied, "What do you know? You are exhausted and on drugs!" She smiled, and I kissed her forehead.

On August 7th, Mary Jo willed herself another day of life. It was her granddaughter's birthday, and she refused to pass on that day. However, the following morning I received a phone call from the nurse that Mary Jo was on her journey and was mouthing my name. I immediately ran over. Mary Jo gave me a smile as I told her I would be with her until the end. After blessing her with holy water from Our Lady of Lourdes, saying a few prayers, and giving her a ceramic dish that had a painting of Our Lord embracing a person who had just passed, we just held hands for awhile. All of a sudden, she started mouthing what appeared to be the Hail Mary prayer. I told her if she wanted me to say the Hail Mary, she should squeeze my hand. She did. I don't know how many times we said that prayer together; all I know is that when I would take a rest, she would squeeze my hand again. At nine o' clock that evening, I felt my presence and her daughter's presence were interfering with Mary Jo's journey. We decided to go home and asked the nurse to call us when she felt Mary Jo was getting closer to God. At 10:55 p.m., the phone rang. The nurse said that Mary Jo was taking her last breaths. It took me mere moments to get to Mary Jo's front door. I ran in just as the nurse walked out of Mary Jo's bedroom to inform me that my dear friend had just passed.

Mary Jo's mission on Earth was accomplished. As she told me two years ago, "It was God's plan for us to meet," and I was to be there for her when the time came. I miss her dearly.

As much as I hope my mission in Florida is coming to an end, I will not question His plans for me. I have always followed his signs, even when I hoped for another. "Let Thy will be done, not mine."